A Mask and Some Talking Leafs

Janet Malcolm

Janet Malcolm

ISBN: 0-9988513-2-9
ISBN-13: 978-0-9988513-2-7

A MASK & SOME TALKING LEAFS

My Story comes from my heart. It is my way
of sharing and saying Yaw^ko (Thank You)
to all who have crossed my path and encouraged me to go on with life. . .

Tewataw^yle

*** AN INTRODUCTION TO THE TITLE: ***

A Mask and Some Talking Leafs

This Talking Leaf is written with the experience of 30+ years into sobriety. I am not a trained counselor, nor is my case exceptional. However, I had a burden in my heart to share my journey because of the gift of survival I have been given. My story is written with only the hope it may somehow strengthen your journey. Yaw^ko (Thank you)

Though the first chapter focuses on shameful experiences, I want to reassure you I have had many more positive experiences during the last 16 years. I am grateful to be alive and living today and for the last two years, this book has been calling out to me. I am a Disabled Viet Nam Era Veteran, a grateful alcoholic, a proud Oneida (Native American), a proud mother, aunt, sister, daughter, and I suffer from bouts of depression and PTSD. Through this book, I hope to share enough of myself to make a difference in your life.

My title mentions a Mask and refers to the faces and fronts we wear. Some masks are healthy and some are unhealthy. People tend to wear a mask for various reasons we may never understand.

We are all survivors of our past. Some struggles, all too numerous to mention, which include layers of shame, guilt and different degrees of pain and self-forgiving. I do not mean to imply we have all lived or survived the worst of life. Yet, what may be brushed off by one person could be devastating to the next one.

Examples of mask wearing appear in the forms of disease, such as covering-up inappropriate behavior, knowing better, but unable to do well and we may even use a mask to get to the next day.

Did you ever notice how people are very good at directing attention to other people or issues? This is another way of wearing a mask of denial. This type of behavior permits us to think other people or issues appear much worse than we are. Usually, low self-esteem or low self-worth has something to do with it.

By belittling someone else, we feel temporary relief because it makes us feel better about ourselves. This places us in an unending cycle. The next time we feel down, we may buy something to make us feel good again. Then another down time, and we find something else to relieve our mask.

*Denotes a Down Day and a time for a new mask. Do I see a negative cycle in my life? Are there any hidden issues I should deal with?

This book describes some of my personal lessons I have learned during my sobriety and I feel they have kept me going when the unrecognized depressions would come. If any of these teachings do not fit your norm – it's ok. You have the right to your own values and I will respect you for your ways. However, if my experiences should get you to start questioning some of your behavior, I strongly suggest you talk to a trained counselor. It's not a weakness to see a counselor, sometimes we just don't have anyone to confidently confide in.

The idea of using Talking Leafs came from a loved one. We exchanged letters for several years and we shared our lives through written pages. He called these letters Talking Leafs. Later in the book, I described what a Talking Leaf means and the benefits you can get from your own Talking Leafs.

Our Talking Leafs gave us the strength and time to build trust in our relationship. I could not trust enough to share my inner most shameful memories with anyone. Through our Talking Leafs we both found ourselves sharing our lives and eventually we came to trust each other enough to talk about our shameful acts. I discovered (perhaps I can say WE) discovered the courage to share firsthand what happened in our lives. He was not a counselor, nor am I. We risked taking off our masks and we discovered what unconditional love was about. Sharing through our Talking Leafs and then sharing through our conversations build up enough trust to take off that final mask. Like I said, our friendship and trust has been building for three years, and it has been worth it. I know we will be life-long friends, if not more...

I remember the teaching that said we have an open door to let the world see part of us, behind that door lays a Mask of secrets and one more door to our sub-conscious. We must learn to open the first door wider so we can get to any dysfunctional thinking and rid ourselves of any misdirected shame.

Remember, "We're as Sick as Our Secrets"

*** CHAPTER ONE ***

My First Journey - One of Many

"THE TRUTH WILL SET YOU FREE. BUT FIRST IT WILL MAKE
YOU ANGRY"   Anonymous

My journey includes some details of my life that I have not even shared with my most precious family. Yet I come to you in hopes that if you should read any part of my story, and see that it may be a reflection of your life, perhaps you can get some help now, rather than wait 16 years as I did.

As a young girl, it always seemed I was the fattest and tallest kid in school. You know the kind, the one nobody wants to pick for their team or the last one left so the team automatically got you. I saw my girlfriends going horseback riding and roller skating without me. I couldn't fit into one of those cute little roller skating skirts and I was just never invited.

Recently I had a dream of meeting Carol, a grade school friend. We greeted each other warmly and went on our way to school. Suddenly, there were all fat and very large students all around us. They were laughing and carrying on like they didn't have a care in the world. I woke up with the feeling that though I thought I was the tallest and fattest kid in school I was so wrapped up in my low self-esteem I just didn't notice I wasn't the only teen-ager struggling out there.

My dream book states that dreaming about fat people predicts a happy life of few worries and many pleasures and that the fatter you (or others) were in your dream, the better the omen. Kind of ironic isn't it!

When I was about 12 years old, we lived in the country. One afternoon, I left a friend's house and was walking home. A man stopped his car and was asking for directions. He coaxed me to his car and there was he was in full glory. At 12, I did not understand indecent exposure. I ran home, no one was there and I hid under my bed all afternoon. In that darkness, I turned the incident into shame and guilt on myself. I did not understand what happened. I just knew that I felt a sickening feeling in the pit of my stomach and in my head. I felt then, that this must be my fault. I carried this misdirected shame and guilt until I was 34 years old and went into a treatment center and found the nerve to tell someone what had happened.

By the time, I got in high school my self-esteem was already low. I had a part-time job at the local drive in. I was bored with school but realized I would not be able to support myself on those wages. So I stayed in school and got my high school diploma.

After graduation, I wanted to see the world. I had remembered I had an aunt who served in the military and at that time, if you weren't 21, you needed both parents' signatures to sign up. I had seen Elvis Presley's army movie and knew that was the life for me.

I had asked my dad if I could join the Army. He said no. he had been in the Marines. At this point, I can only imagine there was too much partying going on even for him. So, as young daughters will do, I bugged him until he finally signed the papers.

What I did not realize at that time was my dad was an alcoholic. He had been sober for about 10 years and I did not have much of a recollection that his drinking days were even a problem. I feel that my mom hid or protected us from a lot of the chaos that went on. The reason why I think that is because after I was into my heavy drinking days, I always felt uncomfortable about entering a tavern when I was sober. Of course, this uneasy feeling left me with the first drink. That uneasy feeling came because I did not grow up in a tavern or drinking scene, so my mom was right about "protecting" us. It had its long range effects. Perhaps, it's time to take a look at the family environment you had or are giving your children. Thanks Mom!

Dad started drinking the summer after my high school graduation. About one month before I was to go in the Army he got picked up for drunken driving. The police told us he hung himself with his belt in the jail cell. Today I still wonder about the details of his death. I am under the impression that all prisoners had their shoe laces and belts taken away.

I couldn't believe it was my dad the police were talking about that night they rang the doorbell. I begged and demanded my mother to let me go to the morgue with my brother-in-law. It was a terrible night. I took on guilt for his death for many years after that because I did not understand the stages of alcoholism. I thought my dad killed himself because I made him sign my army papers. After all, he did not want me to go.

I left for my army training one month later. However, at that time, I too was an alcoholic and didn't realize it. Several nights before I was to leave for Ft. McCullen, Alabama, I went out drinking with some friends. I drove home, I blacked out before I got to our driveway and just drove straight to the river without remembering it. I was awoken by a terrible jolt and an awful sound. I opened my door, and as drunk as I was, I was still surprised to find my feet in the river.

I had fallen asleep at the wheel, and the car went between the bridge abutment and the dead end barricades and that's how I landed in the river. It was a good thing I had fallen asleep on the seat because I clipped a telephone pole and it came through my front window right where I had been sitting.

Again, irrational thinking took over. I got out of the car and walked home. When my mom asked where my car was, I told her I left it on the road because I didn't want to wake her and went to bed. Next thing I knew, there were police flashlights and ambulance attendants in my bedroom. The police were asking me if I was hurt and what had happened. They were already provoked with me because I found out later they had already dragged the river looking for me. I wanted to laugh because I was so scared, but I saw my mother crying. I felt so filled with shame for being the source of her pain, all I could do was hang my head.

I did finally get to Ft. McCullen for training, then to Missouri for a year and spent the last two years at a NATO headquarters near Brussels, Belgium.

Those two years were exciting because I got to see a lot of France, Belgium, Germany and Holland. I was always drawn to cobble stone streets and old castles in my history classes. But along with the sight- seeing, I managed to drink heavily and party for two years- actually all three of my army years.

I met a very nice German sergeant while stationed in Belgium and got engaged. He was very handsome, yet I knew deep inside me I would not make a good wife. I couldn't pinpoint my (alcoholic) problem, I just knew I couldn't get married and I came home. I can see now, I saved this man from a lot of grief. And who knows, perhaps I saved myself from a lot of grief – after all, if I was a heavy drinker maybe he was too.

After the Army, I started to attend the Technical College in downtown Milwaukee. The Salvation Army Center was around the corner. I found myself occasionally driving past the building looking for my dad. I was still in denial about his death. I thought perhaps, it wasn't him at the funeral and maybe Dad was roaming the country as a homeless person. Then I could talk to him and ask him "'why he left us".

Shortly after this, I told myself – I must be crazy. Dad really did die and he really did leave us. I ended up dealing with the misdirected guilt and accepted his death 12 years later in a treatment center.

So if you should ever think of suicide, I would like to comment, you would not be solving the problem, you would only be passing it on to someone close to you. We do not realize it at the time, but we are special to someone and they do need us here. Get some help if you should ever have <u>any</u> type of self-destructive thoughts.

Two years later I married a man from my home town. We stayed married for ten years and had two beautiful children. I never asked him what he thought of our marriage, I just knew it was hell for me because of my drinking, blackouts and the depressions. And by this time, I had more than enough shame and guilt in my life to last several lifetimes.

We separated when our daughter was six months old and our son was not quite two. Being on my own, really gave me the chance to drink. I ended up with my first suicide attempt. I had laid a pillow down near the car's exhaust and left the car running in the garage. It was a good thing, my aunt stopped by and found me. I ended up in a Green Bay hospital and then on to the VA hospital in Milwaukee for 30 days.

The night my aunt found me she rushed me to the downtown hospital, but they said their hospital was full and she should take me to the county hospital for help. I ended up staying overnight in the Brown County Hospital. It was one visit I don't ever want to repeat. The nurse came in my room and in a very cold voice, asked me if I smoked. I said yes, and then she said, make sure you put your cigarettes in the drawer, or your roommate will eat them. Needless to say as sick and tired as I was that night I didn't get much sleep.

The next morning wasn't any better. There were people in the day room, some were just sitting, some were talking to themselves, and some were just roaming around. Then, I saw an old man in a wheel chair that looked like a child's high chair. His wheelchair had a tray on it, he was wearing a seatbelt and a bib. I also noticed that the nurse was standing there getting after him and told him to leave his sheet on that was over his lap.

I can say now I think this story is rather humorous and I tell it with a lot of humor. I thought, this poor man, he must be cold. Well, as soon as the nurse left his side, he pushed the sheet on the floor and wouldn't you know it, he didn't have anything on. I again knew that as sick and hung over as I was, I really didn't think I belonged there, but if I was there – well, it just was not a good situation to be in. I was scared, really scared because, I couldn't quite focus my thoughts and didn't know if I was ever going to get out of there or if anyone cared.

About 10:00 that morning, my aunt and mom came for me. They had some lady I didn't know. I knew they all knew each other because they talked about the families. This lady kept trying to talk to me but I still could not focus my thoughts and to this day, I am not sure what she told me. All I kept saying to myself is "who is this lady"?

When I was finally released that morning, this lady, who I now know is Marge, tried to hand me her business card and what I do remember is, she told me to call her anytime. All I could think of was who was this lady and why would I want to call someone I didn't know?

17

From the county hospital, I ended up in Milwaukee at the VA Hospital. I was put in a room that was locked every night. I thought, now I've really done it. I always suspected there was something wrong with me, and between these two hospitals and all my shame and guilt, all I could think of was that I must really be crazy. And still, I managed to get drunk on the front VA lawn with some other patients before I left the hospital.

I found out later, there were reasons, why my door was locked. One, they did not want me to leave and harm myself because my suicide thoughts were still with me and the second reason was that I was one of the few women patients in the hospital and it was a precautionary step against any sexual assaults. They explained it as a policy and procedure with new patients that came in like I did. Frankly, I don't think they knew what to do with me – after all I was a woman in a predominantly male hospital.

I came home to Green Bay and started drinking even more. This time, my suicide attempt involved an overdose of pills. I had a severe depression where I couldn't even get out of bed. My husband had called the doctor and got a prescription for me. I took the pills for several days, then stock piled them knowing this would be my chance to do myself in.

I had been drinking all afternoon and when evening came and the kids were in bed, I took all the pills and aspirins I could find. I remember praying that night, "Oh God, I don't mean to be this terrible person, I just want some peace and serenity in my life. Please take care of my children, because apparently I can't". My husband worked second shift, so I figured when I died, he would be there for our children.

I don't remember much after taking the pills that night. I do recall my husband trying to wake me up and then there were ambulance attendants calling out to me from far away. I blacked out and somewhere that night, I saw a brilliant white light. A beautiful shaft of light and that's about all I remember, until two days later when I woke up still in the hospital. I was told later while getting my stomach pumped the only time they could get a response from me is when they mentioned my children's names.

I remember, when Marge tried to hand me her business card, not only was I still wondering who was this lady, but my motor movements were not working well and I remembered my mom taking her business card. I had forgotten about it until I came home.

There on the board next to my phone was Marge's business card. Marge was an AODA counselor and I still didn't think I would ever have to call her.

But I did end up calling Marge several times, usually when I got in trouble at work. I managed to have the house straightened up and the kids clean by the time she came to see me. Marge was not aware of my drinking history and didn't think I was in such sad shape.

At the end of all this, I called Marge for the last time and volunteered to go into a Native American treatment center in Minnesota. I went in with the routine thinking, I will do this for my family to show them I tried, then go home and do myself in once and for all.

My younger sister and her husband took care of my children while I was in treatment. I left my children with the feeling that they were in a loving – caring home because of the nature of my sister. Yet, I also felt it was a burden on my family because I felt my brother-in-law did not understand our family closeness. We were raised to support and love each other and sometimes, like this time, my brother-in-law just did not understand that sort of family support.

One of the most difficult pictures I received in treatment was my son boarding the school bus on his first day of school. My daughter and two nieces were all dressed so pretty and waving good-bye to their older brother and cousin. They all looked so well taken care of – they gleamed. I felt so ashamed again because I had missed one of my children's proudest events and again, I was not there to share this moment, nor was I their caretaker.

The treatment center was where I had my first spiritual awakening, along with some other awakenings. My first night there, I roomed with a girl who they had said was there a month and would be leaving for home that night. I lay on my bed very quietly, just moving my eyes. This girl, who was going home, started hallucinating. She started to see snakes all over the place. I had never seen anything like this. All I could think of was – "Am I going to be like that when I get ready to leave?" I knew I was in bad shape, but yet I just wanted to go home.

After the ambulance came for her, a counselor who also happened to be an Oneida, came and starting talking to me. I was so scared I couldn't move. He reassured me I would not be like that in 30 days. I had high alcohol content and alcohol wears off rather quickly, compared to drugs, which I found out was one of the girls' problems. Drugs have a tendency to hide in your fatty pockets causing a time release. They take much longer to get out of our system and even though you haven't had drugs for a while, they could still come back on you.

That sounded reasonable to me. It took him another hour of talking before I would move off my bed. He wanted me to go into the day room and get a cup of coffee and meet some of the other people. I was really scared, I thought; "are they all like that"?

I found out later we weren't all like that. One girl did come in that week, she was still suffering from a doozy of a hang- over and she limped a lot. Finally they made her go see the doctor. She came back with a cast. She had broken her foot and didn't even know how. And I know now, that each one of us could add our own stories here.

During those 30 days, I learned a lot and the experience changed my life forever. We were educated about drugs and alcohol, along with childhood separation issues and Native American teachings.

One day we had a lecture and I had a burning question about the presentation. I held onto my question until after supper when things had quieted down. I went into the counselor's office and it ended up being al all night conversation. When daylight came, I was exhausted and went back to my room. I had been able to release a lot of mental garbage and got some questions answered. As I lay on my bed, I felt so unusual. I started to think about how I felt, it wasn't fear, gladness, happiness – but when I hit the word serenity, I just started to sob.

I went right back into the counselor's office and asked him what was that all about. He had said, "Jan, you have had your first spiritual awakening." That blew my mind and thought maybe there is hope for me after all.

Another thing happened to me. I learned the stages of alcoholism and in one instant I felt relief. I was just an alcoholic, I was not crazy. And in that same instant, I thought an alcoholic, how could I never have another drink in my life. Then of course panic set in at the same time. I found myself back in the counselor's office and she described the One Day At A Time approach. Of course, it didn't sink in that very day, but these people have been so supportive, I thought I would just start paying more attention to what they had to say.

I found my name on the trip list. There were six of us chosen to spend almost a week near Hurley, Wisconsin. At this place, an Ojibwa couple owned some land in the middle of what seemed a state forest. I believe they were both professors. The husband took the men and the wife took us women and we were taught some of our Native American ways, along with what our roles were as men and women.

I experienced my first sweat lodge and a give-away. We slept in one of the biggest Tee Pees I have ever seen. Their son was the all night fire tender. In the morning, I thanked him for being there. Urban Indians, like me, seldom get a chance to sleep in the wild and it was reassuring to have the fire going all night. Though now, I realize the Fire means a lot more.

When we returned to the treatment center, my name appeared on another trip list. This time, a station wagon took several of us to visit inside Sweet Water Prison in Minnesota. It was quite another experience. We walked into the prison and the iron gates closed behind us with such a final note about it. I made a comment to the warden, and he said, "Yes, and just imagine yourself coming in shackled and knowing you wouldn't be leaving at the end of the day." That was enough to send shivers down my spine.

A Native American parole officer talked to us and let us knows that we would be having lunch and then a visit with the Native American group. Sure enough, we got right in line with all the prisoners, and then we were ushered to a private dining room with our trays.

After lunch, we went upstairs to a rather large room. I was surprised to see how many young Native American men there were. They drummed for us and then we had a Talking Circle. We shared our stories and how we came to be there. Then we returned to the treatment center. I remember how quiet the ride back was. I believe we were all thinking the same line of thought, but for the Grace of God, anyone of us could have been a prisoner, instead of a treatment patient because our stories had a lot in common.

In the past several years, I have been asked to speak to several of the Native American prison groups around Green Bay. I speak of my AA story and make presentations of my Native American culture and history.

I felt very honored at one gathering. A group sang an Honor Song for me. My role was a teacher and chaperone. I told the group I felt very privileged to be working with them because I believe I was one of the few people in the world who constantly saw them sober, on their best behavior and making time to share (traditional) spiritual beliefs. I reminded them, I did not know what brought them to prison but I was always aware of the seriousness of their incarceration, and again felt privileged because I did not have to witness anything from their past. I saw only their best behavior.

Back at the treatment center, a time of panic came over me one day as I was standing outside by the lake. I suddenly felt, I had to leave. I started walking back to the building and by the time I reached the building I found myself running. I reached my room and had my suitcase on the bed madly packing. One of counselors had followed me in the room and started quietly talking to me.

I was assured this panic was normal and that it was a good sign. Panic set in because I became aware of all the changes and healing I would have to do to become a healthy person and this was overwhelming me. I also thought of this feeling of panic and thought of my drinking. I always managed to keep a job and this let me have drinking money and I always knew where to get beer. But having this panic attack when I was sober, made me think of what would happen if this was a panic over not having a drink. I could see myself getting real desperate and I immediately thought of my dad. I somehow came to understand what he had gone through. I then thought I had better stay and see this treatment to the end. It was that day that I awakened to the fact I did need help.

At the end of my treatment, they had ten of us line up in a row. And started to describe what would happen to us as Native American people getting out of a treatment center. **I was lined up as No. 10.**

Number one, you will be drinking in less than 30 days and they went down the line describing what each of our chances would be. Number nine; you are the only one who will have a sober life out of the ten. **Number Ten, you will be dead within a year.**

Again, chills ran down my spine. I thought, NO! NO! I want to be Number Nine! Shortly after that, it was time for me to go home. It was bitter-sweet news. It was so safe and reassuring to be in the treatment center. Could I stay sober outside? And yet, I was so anxious to see my children.

By the way, one of my group members did end up as No. 10. He died an alcohol related death nine months after I came home. It was quite shocking; he had been one of my nightly card partners who became a close friend in treatment. His death convinced me even more how serious my weekly AA meetings were to my life.

I came home, and have managed to be a Number Nine to date. I have left a lot of messy details out of my story; I think most of us can relate to that.

One day after I was home for a short time, I ended up having a frank talk with my mom, sister and brother. I described a lot of what I have just written and also that I felt like my skin, my very soul was turned inside out, examined and put back together again. That was how much of an emotional cleansing I went through. It was a very good talk because we all talked about Dad's death, its impact on each of us and what we remembered of him. I am not quite sure we have had such a gathering since.

I have been very fortunate to have such a supportive family members and friends throughout my life. We have talked one on one and that's how I feel we have been able to keep our closeness. They have accepted my occasional recluse ways in a very diplomatic and caring way. Being a single parent and broke a lot, I did let my false pride and sometimes an unexplainable depression get in the way of family and other gatherings, but I was always warmly welcomed home the next time.

I have shared this part of my life as an introduction to some of the teachings I have gained through the years. My story since my treatment center days has been very rewarding, exciting and at times I have been broken hearted. That's life.

My name is Tewaw'yle. In Oneida, that means She Travels. Maria, a special elder to me and Cousin Shirley, helped me with my name. I was quite excited the day I was given this special name. Thoughts of not only physical travel came to me but also thoughts of spiritual journeys came to mind.

Little did I know that it would also cover my journeys into depression. When I think back in time, I have suffered from depression for most of my life, if not all of my life. We all have incidents in our lives in which we will get depressed. However, when the sun is shining and you find you can't get out of bed or feel on the verge of weeping for no known reason, you may be having a clinical depression and you should think about seeing a counselor or your doctor about it.

Some people think we are depressed because of a trauma we

have not dealt with or because we are feeling sorry for ourselves. This is not always the case. The hurt I feel during a depression is very real. I have tried many things to get away from the hurt. Change jobs and apartments at the drop of a hat. I knew that I was a sober person and have worked long and hard for a life of inward serenity. Then a bout of depression would hit me and I would become a recluse. Hiding not only from the pain, but I did not want my family or the world to see me so down. I did not want people to think, "So what good is sobriety if I am going to be like that". So I found myself moving around a lot and keeping an even tighter circle of friends and few support people around me. I feel that was because I could not explain what or why I was feeling so terrible. I knew I wasn't drinking, so why should I have these terrible feelings inside. Well that's some of the thinking my depressions brought on.

In 1994, I had left Wisconsin for New York. Six months later, I came home. I had gotten married for all the wrong reasons and with a depression that had started before I left New York, and it had me in a very vulnerable state. My marriage lasted 67 days. It was my third marriage. I had several issues going on that would throw anyone into a depressed state. I was bound and determined to get my serenity back and to seriously talk to a counselor about what was going on with me. I was sick and tired of having suicidal thoughts, sick and tired of being a recluse, just sick and tired of all the "bad" feelings I had. I had enough faith in myself to think I was a good, worthwhile person. Yet, the bouts of depression would get me into such despair, that I would start thinking my life, my very soul was worthless to this two-legged world.

I have seen my counselor faithfully for six months and he has referred me to my doctor. I am now under my doctor's care and am feeling very "normal", very well. I am on medication and may have to be on it for the rest of my life, but it is such a relief to perform daily tasks without the hurting and the heaviness, that I will take this illness one day at a time. It has not been an easy route, I have had to change medication several times. And in my counseling sessions, I had to review a lot of my life and my living patterns to see what my struggles were all about. The doctor did confirm I have been suffering from a chemical imbalance and the medication will help a lot. That's why I am looking forward to this coming year. What changes are coming my way?

About a year ago, I asked my brother what he saw in my life

that I should think about changing. He said he did not understand why I moved around so much. And that was a difficult way to live. Because every time I moved I had to start all over again. So I thought about this and agreed I was also tired of this. At that time, I did not realize I moved so often because I was trying to run away from a state of depression. I just knew something was wrong, it hurt and thought for sure a new start would give me some relief.

Libraries and bookstores have many good books on all of these subjects. I would suggest you investigate these, if not for yourself then for your friend or family member.

I will close this chapter for now and hope the following Talking Leaf teachings will help you some way.

*** CHAPTER TWO ***

Last Year – A Risk Taking Journey

For a long time, I thought I was the only person to experience such grief and struggles. With the sharing of my life experiences, I hope to impress you with the thought of how important it is to share even our daily happenings and thoughts. It does not have to be with a two legged. It can be with higher power, through prayer talk or even a taking leaf (journal/letter).

We must always acknowledge the negative feelings and emotions at the time they are happening because they are real.

However, by sharing stories and feelings with other people, we usually find out, "Boy am I glad I don't have their problems, and I only have mine." This doesn't necessarily relieve our problems and negative feelings, but it shows us we are not the only one struggling. If they can make it, so can I."

During a summer camping trip, the entire camp had a rummage sale. I bought an 18'' high world globe for 50 cents. I kept that globe in the corner of my living room for several years. When I would get in a "poor me" mode, I would look at that globe and see a small dot that represented my city. The dot was so small, I knew it would be impossible to get a dot size to represent me and therefore, the globe was my reminder that I was not the only one experiencing this negative emotion and that I was not the center of the world, as I sometimes put "poor me."

Whatever I was going through, the globe was there to remind me how fortunate I really was. I would begin to think of other people and their plights – the starving, the homeless, the lonely, the depressed, etc. and I would start to smile at myself. Then actually laugh at "Poor Me". For the world does not revolve around ME – it revolves around all of us. And somehow the thought of feeling sorry for just me seemed absolutely silly.

We can use these personal writings, as reminders of miracles that have happened in our lives, of the struggles we survived, and for those "down" times when we start to think our lives are hopeless. Use your Talking Leafs while you are learning a lesson and remember this is a time to reflect on our actions and the struggle shall pass. And take time to dwell on the struggle long enough to learn a lesson, so hopefully we will not have to repeat it.

The following Talking Leaf describes how I was feeling one

year ago and how I came to repeat my struggle. When I reread this eight months later, I saw a pattern of starting a new life – so I thought at the time. Today, with the help of my counselor, I am picking up my life at a point where I should have continued on last summer. Yet, several months ago I still did not understand depression or that I was suffering from it or that it could have devastating effects if not kept in check. So here's my Talking Leaf from last summer:

Labor Day, 1994, I have celebrated my 15th year of sobriety. You would think that after all these years I would not be in the situation I am in today. But let me explain further. I am a homeless, disabled veteran today as I start this book.

July 20-26, 1994, our veteran's chapter had the honor of hosting the Vietnam Wall here in Oneida, Wisconsin. I was asked to be co-chair for the event. It took two years of planning and waiting to finally get the Moving Wall here. It was a great community event, over 100 volunteers from the community came forward to help.

The Vietnam Memorial Wall was open for 24 hours a day for seven days. A lot of visitors came, the 101st Screaming Eagles, the National Gold Star Mother and the Wisconsin Chapter of the Gold

Star Mothers, the POW/MIA hot air balloon team, the U.S. Marine Color guard and we were also honored by several of Wisconsin's Native American Color Guards, along with visiting color guards from other states.

There was a lot of detail work that went on behind the scenes and as the months before the Wall actually got here it was very hectic. We all held full time jobs while preparing for the wall, except for our commander who decided to quit his position and get on with the last physical details which included getting the Wall site prepared.

My job was also hectic. Our hotel had undergone a major renovation and the new casino, which is attached to the hotel, were planning a month long Grand Opening. I was also asked to be part of the Grand Opening planning team. And to add to the list, my beautiful daughter was preparing for the Miss Oneida Pageant. Amanda knew her culture and history and this was her second pageant. My mother and sister also helped in getting her outfits together. Amanda worked hard at her traditional and modern talent contests. And it paid off, for she became Jr. Miss Oneida for one year. Of course, her pageant and her Pow Wow crowning happened right in the middle of the other two large events. But this time, Amanda came first in my prayers and support. And I was there as her caretaker.

About two months before the Wall and the Grand Opening, I started to earnestly pray to have enough strength to complete both committees and maintain my job duties. I also prayed for emotional strength to get through the month of July. I asked if there were things in my life that I should change, let me clearly see them before the Wall came, for this would be quite an emotional time for many and I wanted to be strong for our visitors and myself.

My prayers were answered rather quickly. I went into a depression. I have not had a major depression like this in twenty years. I went to my counselor and said I know something is wrong because it's not right to have thoughts of suicide and yet that's where I was emotionally.

I was placed on medication and starting seeing my counselor once a week, with the option to call his office any time I needed his support.

Deep down I thought I just needed support, someone to listen to me. During this counseling time, it was made clear to me, that I was not doing things that I wanted to. I was in a give-give situation all around and there was too little receiving.

I had a wonderful job at the hotel, yet my heart was for the culture and history of our people. I had been at the hotel for a year and half, in which time, I started as an Administrative Assistant to the Food and Beverage Manager, the Hotel's first concierge Catering Manager and a part-time historian and cultural advisor for staff meetings, writing descriptions for the Cultural names given to the three restaurants, and writing descriptions for Iroquois designs used on place mats and uniforms.

Three years before coming to the hotel, I was on the Oneida Nation Museum director. I enjoyed learning about our culture and our history, working with the Smithsonian, the National Park Service and area museums. My goals did not "fit" in the higher management's goals and I left one of the most rewarding jobs I ever had.

One thing I noticed about some of our people is that they have not learned to let people leave in a dignified manner. Instead of working with someone's strengths, and giving them the option to working in another area when the position has outgrown them or when they have outgrown their position, the tendency is to not ease them out, but literally cut them out.

My counselor reminded me of many lessons I had learned and was not practicing in my life. The first habit, I had dropped were my daily prayers and I believe I did a nose dive right into the depression I had asked for. It's a good reminder, think about what you pray for because you're liable to get a fast answer.

By the time the Vietnam Memorial Wall came, I knew what I had to do. It was in my mind to write this story and get back into a cultural position of some kind. So I quit my hotel job and was free to finish my duties at the Wall in a calm mode.

I made a two month advance payment on my car and rent, decided to start writing and here I am.

After the Wall left I was able to take an eight day vacation break to the Crow Fair in Montana, see some mountains, the plains at night, stop for a short visit in Eagle Butte, South Dakota and our final stop was in Mitchell, South Dakota at the Corn Palace before coming home.

This trip was important to me for I knew it was going to be a healing trip. The day I left for Montana was the day I threw out my "happy" pills. I knew in my heart, that I was going to make it. I took the risk of again praying, to bring out the fear or whatever it was that I had to come face to face with so that I could once again walk in balance.

My house lease was up the end of August and I decided not to buy this home until I got my head clear as to what direction I wanted to take in my life. I did not feel good about leasing this house. It was a nice small house with a barn in the back yard and I lost over $1,000 in house repairs. I thought I was going to purchase it. It was at this time, I decided not to take another apartment. I was fortunate to have a close family. My mother, sisters, brother and aunts/uncles would have taken me in if I had asked. But I did not want to leave my community, nor become a burden, nor intrude on anyone's space. Talk about false pride!

I took a long shot at the casino, hoping I would win the "big one", this left me almost penniless. I should have known that being the compulsive person I am, the casino was not the place for me. I wanted the easy way out.

I went back to fasting, praying and doing "an honest days' work". I was fortunate the Hotel hired me back on a part-time basis and I was able to pick up some gas and food money while I started to write my story. My cousin, who is so understanding and patient with me, let me stay in her summer trailer and that's where I am writing today.

My two month self-re-creation time is almost over and I have just applied for a cultural preservation job in New York, where our original home lands are. I took the risk of stopping my life to look at and to analyze my professional and personal relationships. And I can only thank the Creator for the results.

Though I don't know the outcome of that job today, I can only say, I feel so much more in control of my life. My friends and my family may not like or even recognize me, but I sure like me again. Welcome home, Tewata'lye.

P.S. While we stopped in Mitchell, South Dakota, I had only enough funds for gas and food and a few extras. I met a man there. He was a professional photographer who was taking an extended vacation across the United States.

I did not have a camera and yet I saw a buckskin dress that I had had a dream about. I asked him to take some photos of that dress so that I could make one similar to it. Perhaps, he will read this and mail me the photos. Note: To my Friend, I have your name in one of my journals and just wanted to say, that by the time you read this, I will be able to afford for the postage and developing. I hope you don't forget me.

Yaw'ko

P.S.S. Here I am one year later, typing my final draft and I found this journal entry and wanted to share it with you. That man did send me several very nice photos of my dream dress. Thank you for remembering me. And as far as just needing support, I now realize I also need my counselor and the importance of continuing my medication even after I begin to feel better. This story is another reason why I am looking forward to this year – now, I feel I have learned several valuable lessons.

*** CHAPTER THREE ***

<u>A Week of Daily Talking Leafs</u>

When we want to change our ways, - it involves taking on new habits. This is not always easy, because it means work and change. Change is work and you know how easy and comfortable it is to continue on just as we are. Think about this. If you write with your right hand, try writing with your left hand. It can be done, but will generally need a lot of practice.

Talk about change. I once asked my Aunt Rose, "How did you get into pottery?" she is a master potter and teacher. She told me she was a legal secretary but when people would ask her what she did, she would say she was a potter. And eventually her dream became a reality. I remembered this story and I want to thank Aunt Rose for her encouraging words, because I took her words and started to tell people I was writing a book long before I even had a format.

I would like to share some of the teachings and lessons I have learned. Again changing habits is a slow process, therefore we shall start out slowly and work at changing only a small part of ourselves. I have written only seven days – a week long journey for you to think about. Each daily writing is called a Talking Leaf. I suggest trying these for several weeks or months until they become a natural way for you. Remember they should only take a couple of minutes a day.

You will notice the daily teachings are listed as Day 1, Day 2, etc., that's because we work different shifts. We have different days off – we do not all work 9-5, Monday through Friday, so therefore this Daily teaching section has been numbered, rather than Sunday-Saturday. You now have the choice as to what day of the week is to be your first day…

Note: Throughout the daily teachings. I have added some prayers and refer to the Creator as GRANDFATHER. I think of my grandfather, his grandfather, my great-great grandfather and I continue to think back until I reach the beginning of all there is – that to me is Grandfather, the Creator.

This is your book, remember you are free to change this name to your understanding.

Talking Leaf One: <u>MY</u> GOODNESS
Did you ever have some good news that you were bursting to tell, yet you had to keep it to yourself, because you wanted to

surprise someone. Take a few moments to think about one of these times. Remember, the smile you wore and the good, exciting emotions you held.

In our fast pace lives, we sometimes don't have enough good strokes in our lives and end up wondering why our lives feel so empty.

So this first day's assignment is to do a kind act and keep it as a secret to yourself. Keep it simple! Save a balloon from a tree, open a door for someone, drop some canned goods off at the food pantry or just simply write a love poem to yourself.

GRANDFATHER, I HAVE BEEN TOLD WHEN WE WANT TO GET CLOSER TO YOU AND TO OURSELVES WE ARE TO TALK TO YOU. MY LIFE, MY VERY SOUL IS SOMETIMES OVERUN WITH NEGATIVE DOUBTS AND FEARS. HELP ME, GRANDATHER TO START TO FILL MY HEART WITH MORE POSITIVE WAYS. WITH THIS SMALL ACT MAY I BEGIN MY JOURNEY TO BE CLOSER TO YOU AND MYSELF. MAY I BECOME MORE AWARE OF THE GOODNESS WITHIN ME INSTEAD OF DWELLING ON THE "POOR ME" PART. Yaw'ko.

Start this new journey out slowly and think about your feelings you experience as you do these small acts once a week. Think of the surprised smile you bring to other people and really think about the good feeling it brings to you. This may be something new to you;

THINKING GOOD OF YOURSELF.

I love steak, and as much as I love it, I cannot share my steak with a newborn baby. The baby would choke. So remember to be gentle with yourself. Go slowly, so you don't choke yourself with while learning a new way.

If these thoughts of self-caring are too much to think about, just start out by performing a kind act once a week. We have a lifetime to think and feel it. After all, we did not become the way we are overnight, so why should we be so hard on ourselves at this time.

Remember to keep it a simple act and write about it in your Talking Leaf so you will have lots of goods works to look at on those days the "Poor Me" syndrome tries to come in.

A Talking Leaf: Examples of my kind acts. How did I feel?

_____

_____

_____

_____

_____

_____

_____

_____

_____

_____

_____

_____

_____

_____

—

Talking Leaf Two: I HAVE FAITH

Today my friend – it's time to reflect on faith – reflect means

to think about, it doesn't mean you have to run right out and get a

religion. If you cannot explain your faith, that doesn't mean you

don't have faith or that you're less of a person, it just simply tells

you, and you never took the time to reflect or think about what you

believe in.

You can start by asking yourself, "What do I believe in?" Is it

someone, or something? There is no right or wrong here, again, just

something to think about.

Your faith is what makes you keep going. If its anger or

revenge, then we have work to do to turn this energy into a positive

force before we get ourselves into trouble. I am not a therapist and I

would advise you to see one if you feel your faith is more negative than positive. Only you can decide this.

Seeing a counselor, does not always mean we are mentally ill or have lost it, again. In our fast paced world, we sometimes just don't have someone we can confide in. we all need someone we can share our ups and downs with. Our lives are constantly changing and we sometimes find we have been so busy, our support system has fallen apart without realizing it.

GRANDFATHER, I AM YOUR CHILD, NO LESS THAN THE STARS AND TREES, AND I HAVE THE RIGHT TO BE HERE. IT IS NOT ALWAYS CLEAR TO ME WHY I AM HERE, YET HELP ME TO NOT DOUBT THAT MY WORLD AND THE UNIVERSE IS GOING ON AS IT SHOULD. HELP ME TO HAVE MORE POSITIVE FAITH IN MY LIFE. Yaw^ko.

Talking Leaf 3: What's in a Hug?

HUG A TREE. Did you ever see that bumper sticker and wonder so what's the rest of the story? I did. So on my lunch hour I started to go to the trees. I would take my shoes off and walk bare footed in the grass and I started to be aware of Mother Earth and her special caring she holds.

I just started to be thankful for what I had in my life – my children, my mother, my family and most of all, the love I could finally feel from them all. Because there was a time, when I could not feel or accept that special unconditional love.

One lunch hour, in my bare feet, I went to a tree and told the tree spirit, I believe you are as alive as I am. I closed my eyes and started to pray and be thankful again, for what I had in my life.

At the end of the week, while I was hugging the tree, I closed my eyes and became one with the tree spirit. And the following poem came to me:

TREE SPIRITS
How Wise You Are.
Patient and ever growing.
Able to change with the wind
And the seasons...
I adore you and how I wish
To be like you.
To have your attributes as a
Constant, Natural way of life
To be ever beautiful and
Changing only on the outside.
To have such strong roots-
So That no matter how
High I go – I remain
Anchored to Mother Earth   Tewataw^lya

This is the day to take five or ten minutes to take a deep breath of fresh air, watch the birds, hold a stone and think of its beginnings. Think of the universe and imagine yourself as just a part of the miracle in the Circle of Life.

Each of us "beings" are unique. The Sky People, the Cloud People, the four legged, the creepy crawlers. We, the TWO-LEGGED beings, have been given free will, a most precious gift.

We do not have to be the center of attention to feel a belonging or to feel loved. Know that by your very existence, you are truly very special.

Talking Leaf 4: In a Rut?

Are you finding life is the same day after day. Well, it's time to be creative. The dictionary defines creative as; to make or produce. What can we create or produce in our lives today to make it a different kind of day?

Let's do something different. Being creative doesn't mean

you always have to do something artistic – but it's been a while since you pulled out your paint brushes or your clay, then maybe this is the day to do it.

I have read that we all have a left brain and a right brain. My understanding is that one side is where our logic and common sense comes from and the other side of the brain is where our creativity comes from.

Perhaps, you have never tried writing, knitting or painting. Today is your opportunity. If on the other hand, these activities appear to be too much, let's look at some other creative ideas.

How about getting up an hour early, and treating yourself to a restaurant breakfast or just driving a new route to work. Think of the breakfast idea as an adventure. Invite a friend or someone you would like to get to know better to breakfast. One day, I found myself in between paydays and couldn't afford to treat myself, much less a friend. So I took the risk of reaching out and explained to my sister, Janice that I would like to do something different this morning. I would like to start the day off with her and could she PLEASE pick up our breakfast tab. This is still being creative because it just might be different for you too. I would not recommend this route too often, for the obvious reason that it does tend to wear on our friendships. And just remember to send a Thank You note.

How long has it been since you visited the library? You know there are all kinds of free information. What if you always had an interest in sailing? Check out a book with a lot of pictures and dare to dream.

Or just write a list of things you would like to do. Putting your ideas or dreams down in writing helps bring them to life.

Nothing great is created suddenly, anymore
Than a bunch of grapes or a fig. if you tell
Me that you desire a fig, I answer you that
There must be time. Let it first blossom,
Than bear fruit, then ripen
Epictetus

GRANDFATHER, HELP ME TO WRITE MY OWN STORY AS I SEE IT. HELP ME TO REMEMBER THAT MY PAST WILL NOT EVER LEAVE ME, NOR WILL THE MEMOREIS GO AWAY. HELP ME, GRANDFATHER, TO FORGIVE MYSELF AND MOVE ON. HELP ME, GRANDFATHER, TO HAVE A CREATIVE DAY. Yaw^ko

Talking Leaf 5: Time for Nurturing

The task for today is LOVE YOURSELF DAY. For some of us, we either have never thought of this or don't do it constantly enough to believe in ourselves. So let's work on this together.

First of all, think about your daily routine. Just make some mental notes of how you think about yourself during the day. Do you hear yourself putting yourself down;

I CAN'T DO THAT…

I WILL NEVER BE THAT GOOD…

I LOOK STUPID, I ACT STUPID…

Pay attention to what you are telling yourself during the day. Get a 3x5 card for your wallet. On this card write positive things about yourself and when you hear yourself saying something negative, get your positive card out and read it out loud. Telling yourself, NO, I AM NOT SO AND SO, I AM THESE POSITIVE THINGS. This is also a good habit to get into when you're not telling yourself enough daily positive strokes to really believe in yourself.

Get a favorite photo of yourself and get it enlarged. Get to know yourself and start envisioning your personality as you want it to be.

I have to tell you a funny story. I went to a Smithsonian workshop and the entire class learned how to do a body mask out of plaster. We ended having our own faces done. I brought mine home and thought one day I would paint it. I haven't got that inspired yet, but I am getting close. By the way, my mask is the picture on the front cover of this book.

But what I did next is quite hilarious to envision. I placed my plaster mask on the pillow next to mine. I have a silver fox fur, which is another story, and laid it over the top of my mask to look like my hair. Then I went as far as placing two pillows for the body and I covered it up with one of my favorite blankets. I talked, laughed, cried and even giggled with myself for two days.

Then it was time for my children to come home and I thought I had better put my other self away because I wasn't quite sure I could explain this event. What I learned from this is that I had fun with myself and it was quite an experience to look from the outside at myself. As you might imagine, I haven't told this story to anyone, so please keep it to yourself.

I don't have a clinical explanation as to what took place

during those two days. I can only say I just really felt more at ease with myself after that. You may not want to try something like this, but take a risk and find your own unique way to express self-love.

GRANDFATHER, HELP ME ACCEPT AND LOVE

MYSELF JUST AS YOU MADE ME – JUST AS I AM.

HELP ME TO BE MORE AWARE OF MY

GOODNESS AND TO BE KINDER TO MYSELF.

TOUCH ME WITH YOUR KIND OF LOVE, GRANDFATHER

BECAUSE MY KIND OF LOVE SOMETIMES GETS MIXED

WITH

SELFISHNESS AND OTHER THIINGS. HELP ME TO

BE MORE LIKE YOU. Yaw^ko

Talking Leaf 6: FUN. FUN! FUN?

A day for fun, perhaps a time to try or to just observe. I have to admit this is one of my most difficult areas. As a young girl I always seemed to be the tallest and the heaviest kid in school and in my neighborhood. Therefore, I spend a lot of time being lonely and alone. And I never really came to enjoy or be good in physical team sports, such as baseball, basketball or parties.

When my own children, were growing up, I had to tell them

one day, that I really didn't know how to be a part of their playing. I would take them sledding and be one of the parents standing on top of the hill instead of jumping on the sled next to them. They would play Monopoly and I would try to play, but it would only last a short time. Somehow, as they grew up, they knew how to have their fun.

The dictionary definition of fun is: A source of amusement, enjoyment, or pleasure. Playful, often noisy activity: To behave playfully; Joke.

Word History: The word fun meaning "amusement" was probably quite new in the 18th century, for Dr. Johnson records it with disapproval in his dictionary, which was published in 1755. Fun is very likely a borrowing of a dialectal form of FUN, "to make a fool of, to be foolish", which has become obsolete in the standard language. The past participle of FUN, originally spelled fonned, has become the Modern English world fond. So there, I think I have procrastinated quite well here.

And it is time to talk about having fun today. I enjoy laughing a lot with people, whether we are playing cards or just visiting each other. I found out, as an adult, I enjoy my sister's swimming pool. The family gets together and we splash and play ball just like kids. I also found out that I still don't enjoy participating in competition games, but I do enjoy watching them.

Are you having fun in your life? Perhaps you can just start by being aware of what you enjoy doing. Then ask yourself, "Am I doing that?" and if not, "Why not?"

"The greatest part of our happiness or misery depends

On our dispositions and not on our circumstances."

Martha Washington

GRANDFATHER, YOU GAVE US A

FUN PART IN OUR LIVES. HELP ME

REMEMBER LIFE IS FUN AND HELP ME

TO EXPERIENCE FUN TODAY. Yaw^ko

Talking Leaf 7: Day A Quiet Time

Sit quietly today. Be aware that you don't have to be the center of attention. People will come to you. However, if we are constantly demanding attention, how would we know that our loved ones or anyone would come to us?

During my month in treatment, I was asked to <u>just sit</u> in the day room. I was always acting up, telling jokes and doing cutesy stuff to bring attention to myself. I asked, "What should I do while I am just sitting there? The reply was "Nothing. Just be aware of what happens." So I just sat in the day room all day, and sure enough friends and other people I had never noticed came and talked to me just to see what I was doing and most importantly, how I was doing. They came to just sit with me and to just be there.

This lesson makes me laugh today. Finally, in treatment, I so desperately wanted to be a sober, serene person that I was willing to try anything. I sat with full gusto. I was so nervous, I sat very rigid at first, trying to make myself that invisible little mouse. I thought my job was to observe other people. By the end of the day I realized people liked me, they came to me. I didn't have to be the center of attention. The reason this memory makes me laugh is I can visualize the counselors watching me around the corner, sitting so rigid and waiting for who knows what.

This quiet time brings two lessons. Be quiet to learn to know yourself. Be quiet and learn that people will come to you. If we keep on the go, we will never learn these good works are within each of us. About three years ago, I had the chance to visit Norfolk, Virginia. I went with my sister, Janice. We enjoyed the beautiful city and got the chance to bond as only sisters can. It was another special time together. My dad had died when I was 18 years old and mom had mentioned that he had been stationed in Norfolk when he was in the Marines. It was a nice feeling to reminisce about Dad and I looked about the city trying to imagine what he saw and what he did.

Our hotel room faced the Potomac River. One evening, Janice and I were on the balcony enjoying the late evening air and watching the city lights glimmer on the river. She told me all we ever need is right here. Water to drink and get our food from. The stars are to study and to read and they will give us light and direction. The trees are for our food and shelter. And we even have the crickets for sound. What a beautiful lesson she shared with me.

This reminded me of another teaching. We all have needs and

wants. Our needs are clothing, shelter and water. All the rest is "wants". Am I letting my "wants" get out of control today?

Be gentle with yourself, if you should find it uncomfortable sitting quietly for ten minutes today, then try it for one. And increase your time slowly. You may find it helpful to get a guided mediation tape to start with.

By sitting quietly, we will get closer to the Creator and to ourselves. This is called internalizing our "Walk", so that we are not just "Talking our Walk".

So take some quiet time, no TV, no radio, no music. Learn to listen to yourself and for Grandfather. If it is uncomfortable for you to do this, ask a friend to sit quietly with you.

GRANDFATHER, TEWETAW^YLE SAID

TO SIT HERE QUIETLY. I DON'T KNOW WHAT TO THINK.

I DON'T KNOW WHAT NOT TO THINK.

HELP ME, GRANDFATHER TO LEARN AND FEEL YOUR LOVE

AND PROTECTION THAT HAS ALWAYS BEEN WITHIN ME.

Yaw^ko

(This is the beginning of the awareness of unconditional love. Did you ever notice how we can scold or spank a child, and yet the next moment, their little arms are lovingly around our necks. Grandfather is the same. He patiently waits for us to take the time to acknowledge Him.)

*** CHAPTER FOUR ***

Beginning Your Talking Leafs

Now it's time for your very own Talking Leaf. This involves keeping a personal journal. And the next question is, "But why". I have found a journal valuable for several reasons. First, when I write something down my thoughts become real. Though, they may be very private thoughts, they are "cemented" in my life and I discovered they are like a road map as to who I am. I have discovered some of my own personality patterns.

I suffer with periods of depression. It could be a beautiful sunny day, the bills are paid and my family and I are doing just fine. And suddenly I hurt so bad inside, the hopelessness I feel brings on ideas of suicide and I find myself making rash decisions and hoping a change will bring some relief. Depression is real. It's like people having seizures, though there is no warning. Recently I have learned to read the signals and most all I have accepted this part of my life.

Though my journal writing did help me tremendously, I did end up seeing a trusted counselor and a doctor. I live a sober life, and believe myself to be a good person and therefore it was really frustrating as to where or why this deep and real feeling of hurt came from.

I think for years my family wondered about my behavior. I felt so bad inside, I didn't want them to see me in this state and I would become a recluse. I would isolate myself, and yet when I did have to go out in public, I would wear a big smile and I don't doubt that if you asked the community what type of person I was, they would say congenial.

And for the most part, I am a contended person but then I would get hit by a depression, in which I would have no control over. Since I have come to accept this part of my life, I take my medication seriously and constantly. You know how most of us are, we feel better and so we quit taking the medication.

Though you may not experience this serious of a setback in your life, your journal will help you see your patterns. Some people have a hard time during the Holidays, or in the different seasons of the year and are not aware of why or that they are even having a difficult time.

I have been told that after experiencing the loss of a serious relationship, through death or separation, we should give ourselves a year to recover. I asked why and was told that each season, each holiday and even special foods will bring out memories and grief and that we need this time to heal from that loss.

Your journal writing will be a source of release for you. I have been taught over the years to write letters to people I am angry or bitter about. Though I never mail these letters, the writings do make me feel better. My dad died when I was eighteen. It was a violent alcoholic death, on that took 16 years to understand and accept. I wrote Dad a letter and said many of the things that I came to understand about our illness and how I forgave him for leaving me like he did.

As babies, we are cuddled and oiled like there's no tomorrow and if we were lucky we had parents who took time for us and listened to us. As adults, we sometimes forget to nurture ourselves. By having your own Talking Leaf, you can learn to take care of a lot of your own needs.

I was told that if we compare ourselves with others, we could become vain and bitter, because there will always be greater or lesser persons than ourselves. We must learn to love ourselves. Our Talking Leafs will let us have a one-to-one relationship with ourselves. After all, if we can't love ourselves, how can we expect to have any other loving and meaningful relationships?

My Talking Leaf: Day One

Date:_____

_____

Time:_____

Weather:_____

The season is

_____

____

(Pick one and start writing how you feel)

I am trying this Talking Leaf because:

Today I feel:

I would like to tell:

Get a coffee mug with your name on it.

Some include a description of your name.

This will be a good reminder as to how special you are.

My Talking Leaf:

Date:_____

_____

Time:_____

Weather:_____

Today was a

_____day

because

Today, I felt

The last dream I remember having was about

    Write your dreams down. They will speak to you. There were times when I would wake up and swear I did not dream anything – I just did not remember. Then I started to ask in my prayers for remembrance of my dreams and have included them in my Talking Leafs.

One example, the time I woke myself up chuckling, gurgling and laughing all at the same time. Of course, this also happened while in treatment (another Awakening). This was my dream: I was in a wooden shack with John Wayne. We had found the person he had been searching for and in that broken down shack, he pulled his gun out and aimed it at the third person. I remember feeling very scared because I was standing so close to that other person and was about to see someone shot to death. What happens next still brings a smile to me – John Wayne shot his gun off, but instead of a bullet coming out of the gun – a red flag reading "BANG" came falling out of the gun, and all three of us just started to belly laugh and that's how I woke myself up. Why was I given this dream? I think it was because I was being all too serious about myself. So far that has been the only time I ever woke myself up laughing out loud and it was quite a funny experience, in more ways than one. So ask to remember your dreams – maybe you will wake yourself up laughing someday.

Now I remember another laughing episode I experience with myself. I had been sober almost a year. Peter, my son, and Amanda, my daughter were so young and precious to me. They taught me to feel unconditional love.

My life as a single parent and a young new sober person was in a rut. I found myself doing all the right things of course. Going to work, attending regular AA meetings, making sure the kids were loved and cared for. They were so young and I couldn't always afford a babysitter, nor did I really want to leave them. So I stayed home a lot and after they had supper, I would exercise or read in the living room.

One evening I felt extremely depressed. Amanda and Peter were eating their supper and I went to the kitchen sink to make it look like I was busy doing dishes. I was crying quietly at the sink, thinking of that song, "Is that All there is?" The kids got their bath, prayers and off to bed they went. I still felt so lonely and empty. I got on my knees and just started praying...GRANDFATHER, I AM TRYING HARD DOWN HERE TO LIVE A GOOD LIFE. I MISS MY FAMILY AND MOST OF ALL, ALL THE LAUGHING WE USED TO DO. HELP ME GET THROUGH THIS DAY. (I know today, these are all signs of a major depression).

Then suddenly while I was still on my knees, it was like a spirit came from nowhere. The next thing, I knew I was laughing and laughing. The more I thought of someone watching me laugh all by myself, the more I would laugh. I was surely a sight to see that night. I finally had to tell Grandfather, "OK, OK!" I had enough laughing and was quite comforted with the thought that Grandfather was still with me.

One more story I do have to remember to leave some room in this Talking Leaf for you also. I was driving home from my mother's house one sunny day and feeling on top of the world. I talked to Grandfather and thanked him for my good feelings. (Remember, I was a new sober person and letting myself feel and experience high emotions without a drink, was quite new to me). I told Grandfather, I would like to sing to Him "Just like a bird". I asked for His help because I am one of those tone deaf people. Well, the next thing I knew I was whistling just like the most beautiful song bird you ever heard. I laughed with tears in my eyes and said, "Grandfather, I surely do know you have a sense of humor. Yaw^ko".

Today my children have matured into beautiful young adults. Because of my teachings and Talking Leaf stories, I feel we have learned to laugh and open up to each other in such a wonderful way. This is also my wish for you and your loved ones.

These are some of my Talking Leaf stories. They helped me
get through my joys, struggles and depressions because they would
remind me Grandfather is always with me, when I would forget that.

SMILE: it takes twice the muscle power

not to smile. Feel the lightness

come in with your smile.

FEATHER LIFE
I feel life is much like a feather,
Delicate, yet strong…
Perhaps because it carries a good
strong, definite pattern.
And like free will – we can always
Fluff it up and change its looks.
But remember, it will still be a feather
Yaw^ko, Tewata'lya

My Talking Leaf:

Date:_____

_____

Time:_____

Weather:_____

Now it's time for you to write. There are such topics as how you feel about yourself, broken dreams, sleep dreams, life goals, inner most secrets, the people around you...

I visited Niagara Falls one year. I was so anxious to see this natural phenomenon with all its power and never ending water supply. It was everything I expected except I could not stop thinking about how close the buildings were to the Falls. This thought stayed with me until I wrote in my journal and drew a picture of what I felt. I drew the Falls with two hands strangling it. Of all the beautiful natural wonders of the world and the skyscrapers and restaurants were practically built on top of the Falls. I felt at times the Falls were being choked.

Your Talking Leaf does not have to be just writing. It can include pictures and drawings or whatever is important to you. Remember, only you will see this, if you so decide.

I have chosen to leave some blank pages for your Talking Leafs. I know you will want to get your own notebook. I hope you have enjoyed this journey. I have much to be grateful for and one way to show that was to take the risk of writing and sharing my

73

Talking Leaf with you.

My Talking Leaf:

Date:_____

_____

Time:_____

IT IS GREAT TO GE GREAT, BUT IT IS GREATER TO BE

HUMAN

Will Rogers

My Talking Leaf

Date:_____

_____

Time:_____

MADE A LIST OF ALL PERSONS WE HAD HARMED AND
BECAME WILLING TO MAKE AMENDS TO THEM ALL.

Step 8, Alcoholic Anonymous

My Talking Leaf

Date:_____

_____

Time:_____

NO MATTER HOW BIG OR SOFT OR WARM YOUR BED IS,

YOU STILL HAVE TO GET OUT OF IT.

Grace Slick

Date:_____

_____

Time:_____

CREATIVITY IS A GIFT. IT DOESN'T COME THROUGH IF THE AIR IS CLUTTERED.

John Lennon

My Talking Leaf

Date:_____

_____

Time:_____

TIME TO ADD YOUR OWN FAVORITIE QUOTES, OR MAKE UP ONE.

With Love, Tewaw'yle

***   Time to get your own notebook   ***

*** CHAPTER FIVE ***

A Closing Leaf

I cannot say I am living a completely contended life today. I have much to learn and behaviors I want to change, but I am again filled with determination. I am fortunate to be in a career I have always had an interest in. I plan to start the last year of my bachelor's degree in Communications.

I am starting out on a new path, with the medication and a clearer understanding of depression I choose to see my future life, my relationship with myself, my family and friends as a much larger, closer circle.

This book describes a lot of what I went through, and yet I know my family had their share of struggles also. I am hoping through this book they will come to realize even more what their unconditional love and sometimes unspoken support has meant to me. Thank you.

When I was in treatment, my mom and my sister told me how they wanted to be a support to me. So the two of them went to their one and only Al-A-Non meeting. They listened to the stories and when it came their time to speak, neither one could say a word because they were overwhelmed and sad to hear complete strangers talking about the same kind of love, frustrations, anger and resentments that they felt.

But this one meeting worked for our family. When I came home from treatment, I opened up and was able to tell them that's how I felt when I went to an AA meeting. I had attended my first AA meeting in Minnesota while still in treatment. I was in this room full of serene women and they reminded me of my mom. I heard and saw how they changed their lives. I was filled with hope. Why couldn't I see these signs earlier? Our family bonded that day and we were able to talk about many things, including Dad's life and his death.

Shortly after that I was talking to my sister, Janice, about the treatment center. My immediate family did not have any knowledge or experience with the AA program, and my sister was curious how they could turn my thinking around in a month. I tried to explain to her the One Day at a Time approach, but like me, I could see she was not understanding something. So I talked her into going to an AA meeting with me. She said, but I don't need that, I am just curious about what goes on in a meeting. And again, I said come with me.

She wanted to know what she would have to do once she got

there. I said, just listen, and when it comes to your turn, just tell the group you're in town visiting me and that this is your first meeting. That's all. And that's how Janice came to visit her one and only AA meeting. On our way home, she said she felt really guilty about being so nosey. I laughed a little and said I didn't take it that way, I just felt your love and concern. Then we both laughed and decided we won't do that again. We are very close sisters and have tried many different things together since that day, but that was one sharing that took a lot of courage and one I will never forget.

A mask and some Talking Leafs was written because I am grateful for who I am and what I am and have felt for several years that I would like to share my story and Talking Leafs with the wish they may somehow enrich your life. And by taking time for myself, instead of running away, I now have a clearer picture of the self-destruction depression has brought into my life. I feel I have captured a finale to the desire of sharing this part of my story.

Yaw^ko, Tewataw^yle / Thank you, Jan M.

THE REAL CHALLENGE OF SPIRITUAL PRACTICE IS TO WORK WITH THE CIRCUMSTANCES YOU FIND YOURSELF IN, NO MATTER HOW UNPLEASANT THEY MAY APPEAR TO BE.

Author Unknown

P.S. I could not have had my story end like this without the love and support of a lot of beautiful people:

THANK YOU DAD. THANK YOU MOM. THANK YOU AMANDA AND PETER.

Thank you Janice, Carl, Katie and Jessica. Thank you Aunt Reka, Uncle Chris, Uncle Emerson and Uncle Irving. Thank you Shirley, Theresa, Bob, Anita and family. Thank you Giff. Thank you Marge S. Thank you treatment Center counselors and patient friends. Thank you inmates. Thank you Don P. Thank you Priscilla, my "old" Oneida teacher and mentor. Thank you Floyd and family. Thank you Bev and family.

Thank you Dr. Judy W. Thank you Kristen and Marla and Alex and my new Onondaga friends. Thank you George A. Thank you Gary A, Little Man and Betty and the Oneida Veterans. Thank you Loretta.

Thank you Tor and Sue B. Thank you Jerry & Jode. Thank you Grace B. Thank you Lizbeth B. Thank you Georgine. Thank you Claudia and Julie. Thank you Paul C. Thank you Nori D. Thank you Paul D. Thank you Elk's Voice. Thank you Marlene. Thank you Sue and Dolly. Thank you Arlene and Nadine E. Thank you Prof. Fine. Thank you Grey Owl. Thank you Judy G. and Robert Y. Thank you Gordy P.

Thank you Leon H. and Scott H. Thanks Dan and Thank you Mary H. Thank you High Eagle. Thank you Gineen Heffner. Thank you Wilma and Mary. Thank you Joann S. Thank you Arlene and Gordy. Thank you Jude and Jen. Thank you Yakeya'le. Thank you Shining Star. Thank you Ray and family and Gathering Flowers. Thank you Hoby & Joey. Betsy & Ronnie. Thank you Brenda K. Thank you Mike K. Thank you Sonja. Thank you Ceil and Ray K. Thank you Ron K. Thank you Ruth & Sandy K. Thank you Leon Shenandoah and ____

Thank you Todd L. Thank you Gail W. Wayne M. Michelle D. Gordy and Betty Mc. Thank you Pat M. and Barb D. Thank you Grandma Blanche. Thank you Kirby. Thank you Roy & Lida, Russell and Jeanie, Ron & Eyvonne. Thank you Bear. Thank you

Steve and Norean. Thank you Opal. Thank you Shirley and Mark P. Thank you Pam O. Thank you Virginia M. Thank you Albany & Rhonda P. Thank you Matt P. Thank you Vic. Thank you Chester. Thank you Denise. Thank you Eddy. Thank you Jos. & Olivia & Family. Thank you Jim S. Thank you Carol S. Thank you Ben V. Thank you Scott V. Thank you Vernon M. Thank you Bobbi. Thank you Dennis W. Thank you Stan W. Thank you Leon W. Thank you Mary Lou. Thank you Pat. E. Thank you Nick S. Thank you David and Lynette. Thank you Henry, My Special One for being there for me and for helping me with the title.

I wondered about starting this list – I sincerely hope, I did not miss too many names. For the many people that were sent into my life really did help me.

www.ingramcontent.com/pod-product-compliance
Lightning Source LLC
Chambersburg PA
CBHW060139050426
42448CB00010B/2212